WE
THE PEOPLE
CORONADO

Published by Creative Education, Inc. 123 South
Broad Street, Mankato, Minnesota 56001

Library of Congress Cataloging-in-Publication Data

Zadra, Dan.
 Coronado : explorer of the Southwest (1510-1554) / Dan Zadra ;
illustrated by Harold Henriksen.

 p. cm. — (We the people)
 Summary: A brief biography of the Spanish explorer who led an
expedition into the American Southwest in search of seven cities of
gold.
 ISBN 0-88682-182-7
 1. Vàzquez de Corondo, Francisco, 1510-1549—Juvenile literature.
2. Explorers—America—Biography—Juvenile literature.
3. Explorers—Spain—Biography—Juvenile literature.   4. America—
Discovery and exploration—Spanish—Juvenile literature.
[1. Coronado, Francisco Vàszuez de, 1510-1554.   2. Explorers.
3. America—Discovery and exploration.]   I. Henriksen, Harold, ill.
II. Title.   III. Series.
E125.V3Z33   1988
970.01'6—dc19
[B]   87-36524
                                                        CIP
                                                        AC

WE
THE PEOPLE
CORONADO

EXPLORER OF THE SOUTHWEST
(1510-1554)

DAN ZADRA

Illustrated By Harold Henriksen

CREATIVE EDUCATION

CORONADO

There was a time when Spain ruled a vast empire in the New World. The empire stretched across Central America through California, Texas, Florida—and even to the West Indies and the Philippine Islands. The Spanish called these lands New Spain—and they ruled the Indian people who lived there with an iron hand.

It was in the year 1536 that four

men came to see Antonio de Mendoza, the ruling Viceroy of New Spain. Mendoza's heart raced with excitement as the men told a story of incredible treasure. For eight years they had been lost in the wilderness. Somewhere north of Mexico City, they had stumbled upon seven cities of gold!

Viceroy Mendoza began to plot and plan. He knew that Hernando Cortes, the Spanish conquistador, had taken great treasures from the Aztec Indians just a few years earlier. He also knew that a poor Spanish soldier named Pizarro had found a second vast treasure in Peru, the land of the Incas. Now the greedy Viceroy hatched a scheme to find and capture a third land of great wealth from the

Indians. He sent a priest, Friar Marcos, to explore the northern lands.

Friar Marcos visited what is now New Mexico. From a distance he saw what looked like a shining city. His imagination ran wild. It seemed to him that this was surely a place of gold. Indian troubles forced Friar Marcos to return to Mexico. But his story of the "City of Cibola" fueled the Viceroy's greed.

Viceroy Mendoza decided to send his most trusted official in search of the gold. The man he chose was Francisco Vasquez de Coronado.

Coronado was a poor Spanish nobleman—one of many who had come to seek his fortune in the New World. He was born in 1510 and came to Mexico in 1535 with the

Viceroy. He may have been a relative. At any rate, the Viceroy saw that Coronado married a rich woman. Then, in 1538, Coronado was made Governor of New Galicia—now the Mexican state of Jalisco. He seems to have been brave and well-liked, but hardly destined to be a great explorer.

His famous adventure seems to have been an accident of history—a stroke of luck. He did not go out on his own, as Pizarro and De Soto had done. He had no dream of glory like Columbus. Coronado was given a job to do, and he simply did it.

On February 23, 1540, his expedition set out from Compostela, Mexico to find the seven lost cities of Cibola. There were about 300 sol-

diers and gentlemen, another 500 Indian servants, some priests, and a vast number of horses, mules, cattle, and sheep. Feelings of joy and excitement swept the expedition forward. But trouble was on the way.

They were only about 100 miles out, still in country that was supposed to be peaceful, when one officer was

killed by an Indian arrow. It was only a hint of what lay ahead of them.

Now a sense of fear and foreboding descended on the soldiers. The army, guided by Friar Marcos, moved slowly and silently through the rough country. Food began to run short. The heavy supplies were lost or

thrown away by the tired servants. They suffered from heat, thirst, and weariness.

The journey to Cibola was 1,500 miles long. In July, the spirits of the men began to brighten. They knew they were coming closer and closer to their goal. Soon, they would see and touch entire walls of beaten gold. Finally a strange shape appeared on

the distant horizon. "It's there!" cried Friar Marcos, and the men took up the call: "The City! The City!"

But the desert sun had played tricks on their eyes. Instead of a beautiful city, they found only a walled pueblo village, built of mud and stones.

Well-armed Indians refused to allow the Spaniards to enter. Coronado's men were starving and desperate. He ordered them to attack. The Spanish cannon, crossbows and muskets soon overcame the Indian spears and stones. The brave Zuni Indians fled.

Coronado's expedition entered the pueblo. They found no treasure—but there was fresh bread and vegetables. At that moment, food was a greater gift than gold. The men fell wearily to their knees and thanked God.

But where were the seven cities of gold? In the days that followed, Coronado sent parties out to explore the "Land of Cibola." Meanwhile, poor Friar Marcos was lucky to escape with his life. He was their guide. The men blamed the entire disaster on him.

One group of Spanish scouts visited the Hopi pueblos to the northwest. Again, they found no gold. But a captain named Garcia Lopez de Cardenas came back with a fantastic story. He swore he had seen a mighty gorge. So deep was the gorge that the river below seemed like a tiny silver thread.

Everyone laughed at Cardenas. They had no way of knowing that he had actually discovered the Grand Canyon!

Another captain, Hernando de Alvarado, went eastward into Texas. He, too, returned with a strange story. He said he saw vast herds of huge "hump-backed oxen." These, of course, were actually the buffalo of the Plains.

In August, Coronado sent a sad letter to the Viceroy: "The Seven Cities are only seven little villages....There does not appear to be any hope of finding either gold or silver."

But he intended to keep on searching.

Coronado spent the winter of 1540-41 in a village on the Rio Grande called Tiguex. He was there

when Captain Alvarado rode in with great news. An Indian from the North, held captive by a Texas tribe, had told him of a country called Quivira, which was full of gold!

At first, Coronado wouldn't believe it. He had already been disappointed too many times. But Captain Alvarado had brought back proof this time. He still had the Indian captive to vouch for the truth of the story. Coronado nicknamed this Indian "Turk" because of his shaved head.

Turk said he would guide Coronado to the treasure.

In April, 1541, Coronado and his army set out for Quivira. The men were happy and full of hope. Turk told them that it was not too far away.

He told them that the King of Quivira rode in a golden boat and that the people ate from golden dishes.

But as he spun his tale, Turk led the army into the desolate Staked Plains of Texas. A second Indian guide, Isopete, told Coronado they were going the wrong way.

The Turk had to confess. The Pueblo Indians had promised to let him go free if he took the Spaniards into the wilderness and lost them. Coronado was furious but still hoped to find Quivira.

He sent the main army back to wait at Tiguex. Then he picked the 30 best horsemen and six loyal foot-soldiers to go North with him in search of the City of Gold. Isopete led

them. Turk followed behind—in chains.

They had a magnetized needle, hung from a silk thread. This simple compass pointed the way to Quivira. They traveled for 30 days, following a trail made by buffalo. Finally, they came to the swift-running Arkansas River.

Isopete told them that beyond the river lay his homeland Quivira. And as he had also told them, the country was beautiful, with fertile soil and peaceful people—the Indian tribe now called the Wichitas.

But again there was no gold. Turk surged against his chains and cried out for the people of Quivira to murder the Spaniards. Disgusted, Coronado had him executed.

Then he solemnly claimed the land for Spain. The wise old Wichita chiefs just smiled.

It was August. Soon the autumn would come and then the winter. The Wichitas provided Coronado with guides to lead him back. It was a gloomy trip. Along the way, Coronado rode silently by himself. The men knew that their leader needed time to think. By now, he was nearing despair.

They stopped at Tiguex to spend the winter. In December, Coronado suffered a head injury in a fall from his horse. Confused and in pain, he began to long for his wife and home in Mexico. The next spring he led the army home. The priests stayed to convert the Indians to Christianity.

Coronado felt defeated because
he had not found the treasure he ex-
pected. But history would eventually
make him an important figure. In his
futile search for gold, he had explored

the western coast of Mexico. He had discovered the Grand Canyon and charted the route of the Rio Grande. He had gone farther north than other Spanish explorers—through the Texas Panhandle into Oklahoma and eastern Kansas. Because of his bold exploration, Spain claimed a new part of the world and began to settle it.

With his job done, Coronado resumed his governing of New Galicia. But the great explorer was an inefficient governor. In 1544 he was removed for neglect of duty and spent the rest of his life as regidor, or alderman, in Mexico City. He died peacefully in bed in 1554, only 44 years old.

WE THE PEOPLE SERIES

WOMEN OF AMERICA

CLARA BARTON
JANE ADDAMS
ELIZABETH BLACKWELL
HARRIET TUBMAN
SUSAN B. ANTHONY
DOLLEY MADISON

INDIANS OF AMERICA

GERONIMO
CRAZY HORSE
CHIEF JOSEPH
PONTIAC
SQUANTO
OSCEOLA

FRONTIERSMEN OF AMERICA

DANIEL BOONE
BUFFALO BILL
JIM BRIDGER
FRANCIS MARION
DAVY CROCKETT
KIT CARSON

WAR HEROES OF AMERICA

JOHN PAUL JONES
PAUL REVERE
ROBERT E. LEE
ULYSSES S. GRANT
SAM HOUSTON
LAFAYETTE

EXPLORERS OF AMERICA

COLUMBUS
LEIF ERICSON
DeSOTO
LEWIS AND CLARK
CHAMPLAIN
CORONADO